A Trip to Washington, D.C.

Boston, Massachusetts

SOCIAL STUDIES

Min, Fatima, and Ricardo were really excited. They were going on a field trip to Washington, D.C., with their teacher, Ms. Lopez. It was their first time to visit the famous American city. They wanted to learn more about US history.

"Are we there yet?" asked Ricardo. "I've never been to the **capital** of the United States before!"

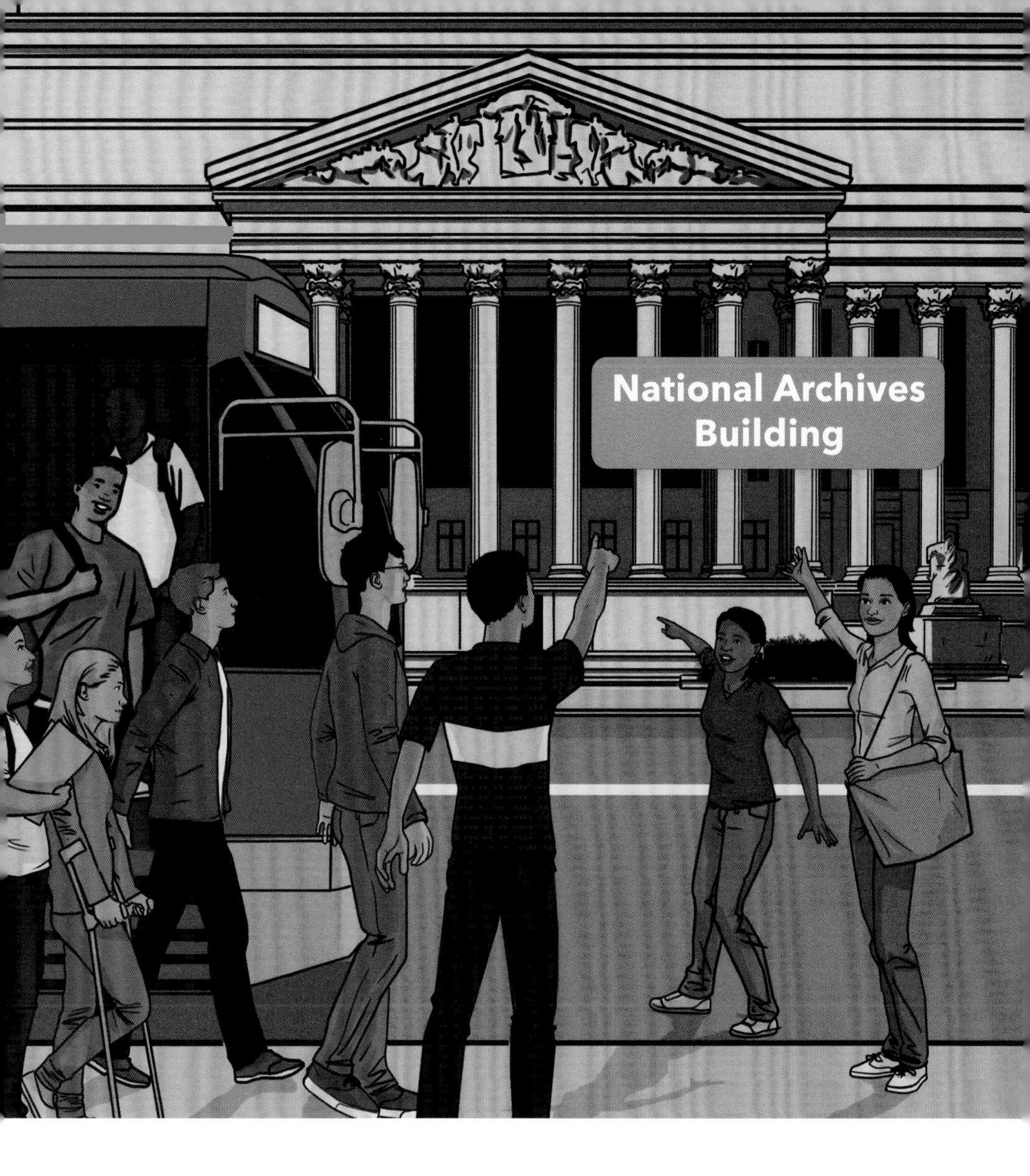

After some time, the bus stopped at the National Archives Building. "OK, class!" began Ms. Lopez. "The **Constitution** is in this building. Who can tell me more about it?"

"The Constitution is the document that sets US **law**," said Min. "It's an important part of our history."

"Correct!" answered Ms. Lopez. "Now follow me so we can learn more."

As the class walked inside, they saw the original Constitution behind glass. The constitution divides the US government into three parts or branches. There is the **legislative branch**, the **executive branch**, and the **judicial branch**. The Constitution also makes it clear that all people in the U.S. are created equal.

"Does anyone know when the Constitution was written?" asked Ms. Lopez.

"A long time ago?" joked Ricardo.

"That's true," answered Ms. Lopez, smiling. "It was written in 1787."

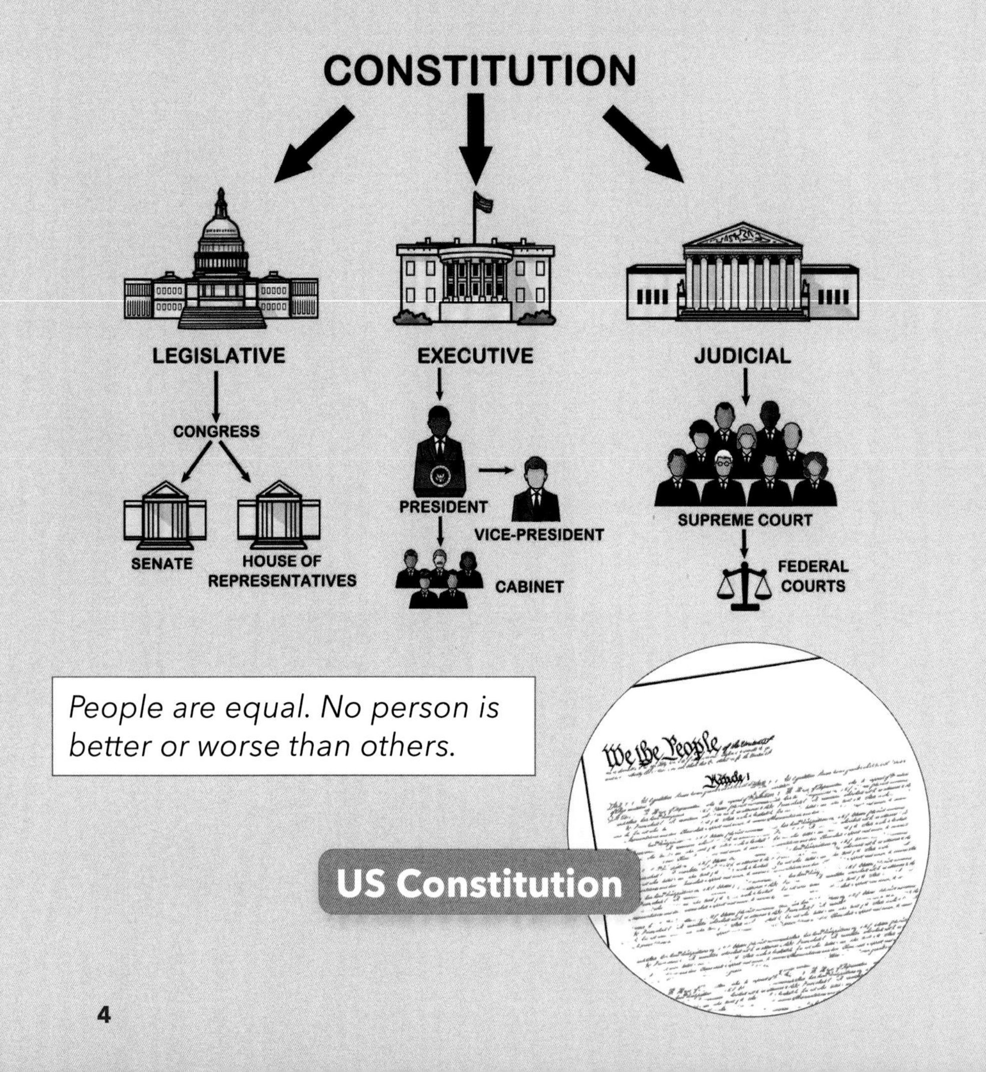

People are equal. No person is better or worse than others.

US Constitution

The class started to read about the different branches. Fatima was the president of her class, so she was interested in the executive branch. "The president is part of the executive branch, right?" she asked. "My brother told me that the president has all the power," said Fatima. "I want that job!"

Ms. Lopez turned to the class. "Is Fatima correct? Does the president have *all* the power?"

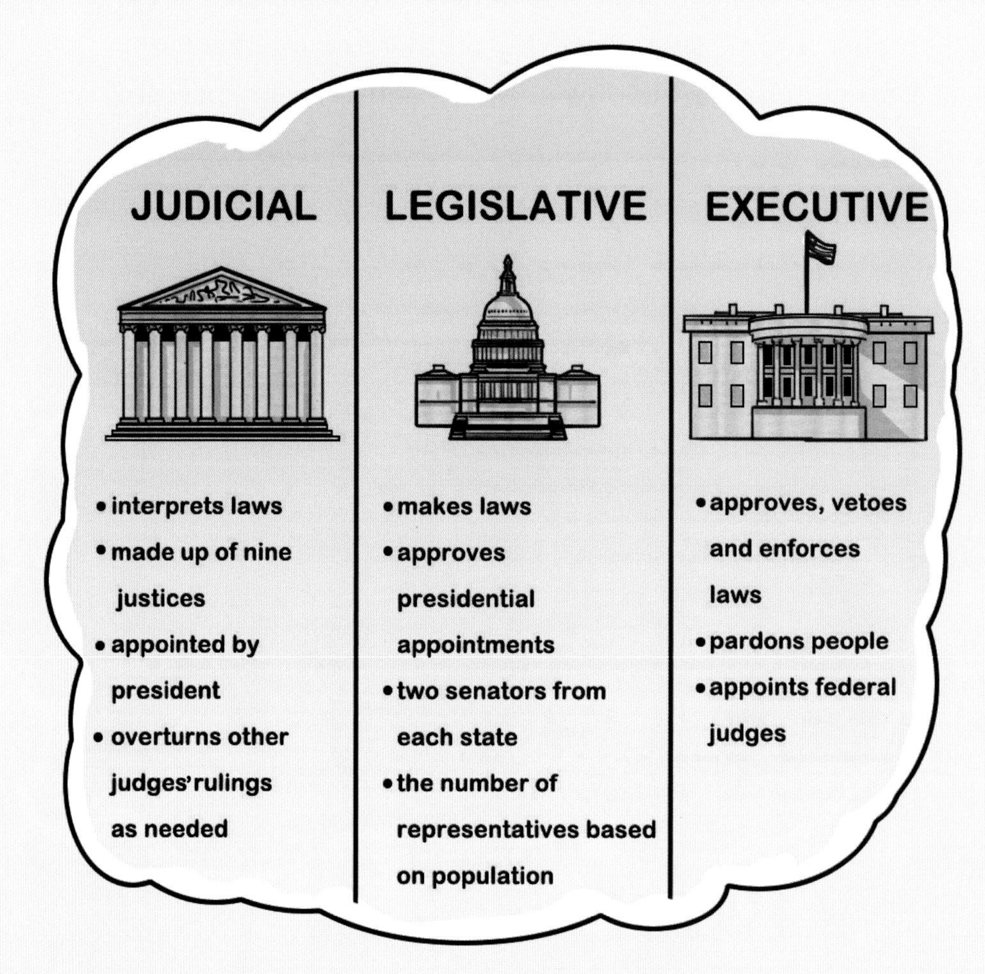

Transportation is related to systems for travel.

Ricardo quickly raised his hand. "I don't think so," he replied. "The US government was designed for each branch to have different, important jobs. It's called **separation of powers**."

Ms. Lopez smiled at Ricardo. "You're right. The branches are equal. One does not have more power than another," she explained.

"Well, I still want to be president!" said Fatima, looking around at her friends. "When I'm president, you can all work in my **cabinet departments**. Maybe you can be in the Department of State, Ricardo? Or Department of Transportation?" Then, she turned and asked, "Ms. Lopez, would you be my secretary of education? You could improve schools across the country!"

Ms. Lopez laughed as she answered, "Sure! Thanks, Fatima."

The class walked to the National Mall. They saw beautiful things everywhere. They saw interesting statues and famous buildings. They even saw the Washington Monument. "This is so exciting!" said Ricardo.

The class looked at the statues of President Lincoln and President Jefferson. They took pictures with all of them.

KNOW IT ALL

The United States **elects** a president every four years. This is one **term**. The same person can be president for two terms, or for a total of eight years in office.

The class walked for a few minutes. Then, Fatima saw a large building with many beautiful flower gardens. "Look, it's the White House!" she called. "The president lives there."

"Wow," said Min. "I've only seen the White House in movies."

Fatima smiled. "Min, you can visit me there in a few years! Maybe you can be my **vice president**!"

"Sure Fatima," laughed Min.

Next, Min saw a large building with a dome. "Hey! That's the Capitol Building," he pointed out. "**Congress** works there."

"That's right, Min!" said Ms. Lopez. "And what branch of the government are they?"

"Congress is the legislative branch," explained Min. "Members of Congress write the laws in the U.S."

"Very good," answered Ms. Lopez. "There are two parts of Congress. What are they?"

"The **Senate** and the **House of Representatives**," answered Min. "Each state elects two senators. They also elect representatives. The number of representatives in each state is different. States with more people get more representatives in Congress."

"Well done," said Ms. Lopez.

Min looked at his friends. "I think that sounds cool," he said. "Laws can help people have better lives. Members of Congress help their communities." Min looked at his teacher. "Ms. Lopez, I want to help people in my state," he began. "Do you think I could be a member of Congress?"

"Of course! That would be great!" said Ms. Lopez.

Min felt excited. He really wanted to help people.

KNOW IT ALL

Members of the House of Representatives must be 25 years old or older. Senators must be 30 or older. The president must be 35 or older.

Finally, the class walked towards another large building with white columns. Ms. Lopez spoke to the class. "Welcome to the **Supreme Court**. It's the highest court in the country. What do you know about it?"

Ricardo raised his hand. "They make decisions about laws in the U.S. They make laws equal for everyone. The president chooses **justices** and then the Senate approves them."

"Good. How many justices are there?" asked Ms. Lopez.

"Nine," answered Ricardo.

"Right again," replied Ms. Lopez.

Ricardo thought about the job. "The Supreme Court checks that laws are fair and follow the Constitution," he began. "Could I be a Supreme Court justice?"

"I think you would be a wonderful justice, Ricardo," replied Ms. Lopez. "There have been many amazing Supreme Court judges in our history. I hope you become one." Ms. Lopez paused before adding, "OK now, class. It's late. Time to eat!"

The three friends sat down to eat something. They were excited about what they had learned. "Washington, D.C., is so interesting!" said Ricardo.

"Yeah," agreed Min. "I'd like to live here someday."

"Why not?" asked Fatima. "We're a good team. We can live and work here. We can be part of the government."

"You're right," replied Ricardo. "We're just learning about US history now, but we *are* the future!"

"Yeah," agreed Fatima. "And we can make the future—and our country—a better place!"

capital the city that is the center for the government of an area or country

Constitution the main set of rules and ideas that created the government of the United States

law a rule made by the government that all people must follow or they will face problems with the police

legislative branch the part of the US government that makes rules for all people to follow

executive branch the part of the US government that makes sure that people follow government rules

judicial branch the part of the US government that checks to see if government rules follow the Constitution

separation of powers the model of the US government in which the work and duties are shared by three different parts

cabinet department a group of people who help the US president do his or her job; special groups that work on different US government issues

elect to choose a person for a job or government office by having people say who they want

term the limited length of time a a government official can stay in a job

vice president the person who is second in power after the president

Congress members of the part of the US government that makes government rules which includes the House of Representatives and the Senate

Senate the US government group made up of 100 members chosen by the people of the U.S. (two members from each state)

House of Representatives the US government group made up of members chosen by the people of the U.S. (the number of representatives per state changes with the number of people who live in a state)

Supreme Court the highest place where people check US government rules

justice a person who has the power to make a decision about government rules; a judge